Your Dazzling Death

Your Dazzling Death

POEMS

Cass Donish

ALFRED A. KNOPF

NEW YORK

2024

THIS IS A BORZOI BOOK PUBLISHED
BY ALFRED A. KNOPF

Copyright © 2024 Cass Donish

www.aaknopf.com

LIBRARY OF CONGRESS CATALOGING-IN-PUBLICATION DATA
Names: Donish, Cass, [date] author.
Title: Your dazzling death : poems / Cass Donish.
Other titles: Your dazzling death (Compilation)
Description: First edition. | New York : Alfred A. Knopf, 2024.
Identifiers: LCCN 2023048512 (print) | LCCN 2023048513 (ebook) |
ISBN 9780593538036 (hardcover) | ISBN 9781524712518
(trade paperback) | ISBN 9780593538043 (ebook)
Subjects: LCSH: Caldwell, Kelly, 1988–2020—Poetry. | Caldwell, Kelly,
1988–2020—Death and burial—Poetry. | Caldwell, Kelly,
1988–2020—Mental health—Poetry | Bipolar disorder—Patients—
Poetry. | Grief—Poetry. | LCGFT: Elegies (Poetry) |
Biographical poetry. | Queer poetry.
Classification: LCC PS3604.O548 Y68 2024 (print) | LCC PS3604.O548
(ebook) | DDC 811/.6—dc23/eng/20231218
LC record available at https://lccn.loc.gov/2023048512
LC ebook record available at https://lccn.loc.gov/2023048513

Jacket art by Kelly Caldwell
Jacket design by Chip Kidd

Manufactured in the United States of America
First Edition
1st Printing

for

Kelly Renee Caldwell

(DECEMBER 26, 1988–MARCH 23, 2020)

I can't confront her face to face; I must take small sips of her face through the corners of my eyes, chip away at the ice a sliver at a time.

—GLORIA ANZALDÚA

and she said it was not up to me
to live without her
or make the voice be single,

she said every voice is needed.

—BRENDA HILLMAN

Contents

***

A NOTE ON THE TITLE

The title of this collection is taken from Marosa di Giorgio's *The History of Violets,* translated from the Spanish by Jeannine Marie Pitas.

Your Dazzling Death

* *
 *

The Question of Surviving This

In my next life

      [since this
one burned
     to ash
that night

      when you shook
yourself
     out of
the world

      your touch
now memory
     an eyelash
on the sink

                your foundation
and blush
     still behind
the mirror
                         ]

I live in a trance,   in a trans-
formed valley,
where the last flowers bloom

and the last dogs eat them. I lower
my mask to eat the last salmon,
suck the last peach, scrape artichoke

with my teeth. The wind licks my face
and licks my plate clean
on days I have no appetite,   every day.

    Let me paint this

        entire country
        the colors of your face
        the last time I

                saw you alive

Anticipation of Spring

There's something about hunger I wanted to tell you
It's impossible to know who belongs to the lake
Until it's drained
Admittedly a swim was desirable and I undressed
Admittedly I went too far
I've been minding the mourning fires
For nearly a year now say it time has ended
Someone found us in the wrong bathroom
We were scared to death
Civilization is here with green buds beating
Our ears while we attend live radio shows and cover
Our mouths with rent garments pretending we know
What to hate
I wanted to say
Pour lake ice over me kiss my blue mouth
I am drinking milk as the earth tilts
More services were suspended today I pulled
My porch sweater over the windchill I spoke
Using someone else's voice on purpose
All or none of this is accidental
I attempt a philosophy or a flower petal
See the wild violets sewn onto my eyelids
See the galaxies creased and set aside like newspapers
See the dogwood preparing to blow into pink flame
The government said come to the town hall meeting
Make your voices heard the government
Said don't leave your homes
My lover bakes smells into the kitchen

She says don't cry the bread already has salt
She says to the mirror you're beautiful and spins around
She says my parents won't say my name
Then she falls on the floor and says I hate you good night
She says I love you and the wild stars
She says it's the cat I hate and the sounds in my head
Listen
The mourning dove will conduct the dandelions
It seems we are all responding more or less to light

Dignity

After an earthquake, my mother would
          rebuild our home, change
her name, give us new

coordinates. See the diamond
          on the map, the pull-apart basin,
see the flashing yellow arrows all

along the San Andreas Fault,
          see unintegrated scenes over years,
how they fell together only

in how things fell apart. Love, I want you
          to know I saw your dead
initials scrawled in dust, but even now,

I hear the mountain goats I sent,
          clacking over them at dusk. We spooned
out avocados beside lakes,

I licked pink salt from your nape,
          drew the shapes of continents
on your back, sounded out

your new potential names
          until we found those syllables
that tasted, you said, like honey—

which tasted, you said, like having
        a future. When we became lovers,
you searched my face as if

something there could be enough
        to save you. Maybe we believed it
for a while, maybe it was true

for a time. I know your name
        gave us years and gave to you
a life to call your own. Now I face the sky

and ache for a different end, a bluer
        hue, a better face. Some say my pronouns
should be used for the plural only,

but my dreams
        are singular: I see the tectonic
plates shift, a humid gust

        slaps me hard: I taste the sweetness
of you on my tongue.

your dazzling death

dazzling as in
        I'm dazed as in
a life's been razed

torn down burned down
        bulldozed
my yard a wasted expanse

dazzled as in
        what dazzles can floor
can devour

dazzled as in
        stupefied   stunned
in a stupor   spun

as in dire   as in
        my history is now on fire
as in I'm reduced to a child

dazzled as in bewildered
        helpless   sprung
unbearably   tired

dazzled as in
        I'm rattled
I'm rambling and tattered

dazzling as in
          so bright I've been
submerged in flame

within it   I come
          and go   I succumb
to the widening gyre

as in your side
          of the bed is a void
your side of the bed is absence

your side of the bed is the horizon
          of a black hole
is horizontal

is the only presence
          as I lie and stare at the wall
it's louder than the world

brighter than existence
          a brighter word than bright
collapsing me into questions

where is your poise
          your twinkling   voice
cutting you to the quick

your beckoning   hands
          with ten moons agleam
your hair loosely braided

you were dazzling
      and dazzled
as in   devastated

Sitting in Again Park, Columbia, Missouri

all things live and die by starlight
under the gaze of the universe
the terrible sun
covered in a thick milk mist

Before it happened, the scenery
was blameless, it swayed
like one of your floral dresses.
Finches sang in the morning,
sang *before, before*—

What would I give to go there, what would I take?

What would I do to find you and eat the fruit?

These roots
where you sat then stepped away
from yourself in the new moon dark,
this tree
is a portal to you.
You
exist—inaccessible, yet
I imagine you

imprinted on my skin,
how you breathed
into my mouth, saturated
my cells with vertigo.

So am I the portal? Do I find you
through myself?

Perhaps a portal
is always everywhere, waiting
for me to look.

I can't look everywhere. We moved in
and toward
each other, but now that life

is suspended
in sugar water,
in *forever*, in smoky quartz—

Grief Song

*Bergy seltzer is a continuous crackling, frying sound
that has been heard by submariners and other sailors
when close to melting icebergs.*

—GEOPHYSICAL INSTITUTE

you drift at breakfast
     like a continent
lose an earring
     in your tea
the sediment
     of a life trans-
fixed in geo-
     logic time
what kind of sound
     was heard at the hack-
berry tree that night?
     answer: the pop
and sizzle one hears
     as icebergs thaw
releasing air
     trapped deep in years
a layer of snow-
     melt in my wine-
glass now fizzing
     at the interface
between your time-
     line and mine

Agate Beach, Lopez Island

Above the cold rush,
        the cliff paths are burdened
with beauty—

how the lichen
        blankets boulders, the Salish Sea
down below and glowing

under a pale sky. I remember you
        happy one summer,
waiting for my orders
        in a pink leather collar.

I'm on the moors in a death novel—

                sandstone, clouds, wind,

                and danger, the love threat—

the violent retreat
        from life after life
is torn away. I don't know

if it's then or now
        anymore. If you're here
or already gone. If the words

I recall have already
        been spoken: *I don't want*
to live. A tsunami

is predicted here,
        could take us all. I don't think
you wanted to die, not that day.

        In another life,
that's how we go: that day,
        together. Torch wave,
fire in the middle

of green. You never make it
        to your other death.
With all these threats

looming—
                more than five hundred
        anti-trans bills
        moving through state legislatures,
        heat in the atmosphere
        and in the sea, glaciers
        unburdening their water—

what would it mean
        to take vows?
To say *the future*—stepping, with the phrase,

toward an edge
        without knowing
what could be underfoot:

flowers, or flames,
or that sudden drop

down to water hard as gravel,
quick as a gunshot.

Via Negativa

My grief is not a gigantic orb
hallucinating, vibrating, singing,

color of lava, color of a forest,
color of night, of the sun,
of a rainstorm,

              of the temperature it was on the day I was born.

It is not the size of a planet.
I don't hold it in my arms hour after hour,

        don't

              let it singe
                 my body.

She turned to baking at her most depressed
and now the fall is empty of the scent.

My grief isn't intimate,
        daily as bread,

hot to the touch,
and burning on the inside,

burning all I've been

I've never   been enough

          to save someone   with only love

Your Illness

You didn't believe in superstition.
Your hands trembled
like an urgent question,

and there
were gaps,

so many, you didn't recognize

our street,
forgot your friends' names

                                        *

        Something in you stirred,
a sadness at first—that's when
it still looked
eager—but then
it was beyond sadness,
you became inert,

one day I found you
lying on the kitchen floor

                                        *

A desolate fire.
It lingered, and sometimes
it mellowed, but then you'd find
it charming; that's when

it was dangerous.
It whipped like a deadly joke.
It sucked on itself like a lemon.
It laughed at water.
You wanted to fuck, and fucking me you said,
I am the greatest lover in the world.

Later you banged your head against the closet door

and I started shouting in fear

*

electroconvulsive inpatient therapy room emergency meds agitation
meds selfharm ideation risktaking behaviors meditation mixed
anhedonia features rapid hypersex cycling catatonia mindfulness
klonopin sleep dysregulated routine meds meds levels meds remission
severe circadian nausea rhythm pressured speech racing thoughts

agitation agitation agitation

*

I   never   wanted   you
                      to   see   you
like that again,
        it scared you, scarred you,

            my darling girl (you loved
            being called *girl*)   my woman

    you mouthed *Help me*
    at the kitchen table

Yet within it,
one thing—
                    one thing

that was always
true, unwavering in all   the years
I knew you—

you said if you had to live
with this
illness,

at least you'd gotten this far:
at least you'd looked   in the mirror
at least once

and knew who you were, felt
whole, knew
you'd lived,

finally
loved and been loved
as you—and I tell you

you are perfect

                    *

Are you clear of it now,
the illness,
in the after

                        a veil
separates us.

I see you stepping lightly on the grass,
barefoot under long black branches

and the light of stars.
You move around, you test

                the air, the new buds,
        to find what you want

me to taste.
So I'll know

                        *

the illness. In a dream
you said it was gone.

All you needed
to give back,

all you had
to give away.

It is time for the day's report. The last peach tree
has died and with it every natural
summer past this June. The last estrogen
they gave you is gone
and you're running. I try to stop
you and fail. I run to the corner in the heat
and undress, trying to wave
you down. I buy a mountain
of shiny limes,
they mold immediately.
So I steal from the corner store:
a carton of grass, unripe bananas,
swollen mangoes, your lithium, verdigris
from an alley. Love, it's about
to rain again. Please believe me
when I say you're the one
on fire. From between two glass panes
I slide out an overgrown live oak
whose lungs could suck up the galaxy.
Your hair fills with ash, but you don't
seem to mind. I look at dozens of images
of Jupiter's moons. I rename all of them:
Loss, Lost, Gone. Sometimes I still think of your back
cool beneath the circles of my palms.

Similitude

I liken you
to a tongue that licks—
a lick that leaves

a substance—
from sea level
to alpine

you were spectacular
after a rain
I lichen you

to a symphony
composed on an organ
[composite organism]

ensemble of colors
variant heating of
earth's surface—

a geologic account—
I lichen you
to rust-colored

rust   dear lichen I like
your color—orange-red
yellow-green [those of your

component organisms]
I lichen you
to flakes that peel

like paint   I like you
to paint
on the exterior

wall of a home—
there you are, as if
a bloom, as if a powder—

an appearance as if
rouged, as if powdered
as if   as if   as if

there you are
on a broken roof
a rocky coast

arctic tundra
desert rock
there you are

on a gravestone
I like you   I'm likely to
     lichen you

I'm ashamed
of how my mind
will strip things bare

with comparison—
I strip you bare
with a name—

reindeer moss
iconic as a name
I dress you up

as something else—
say, moss   say, reindeer
an instant, for instance

or the duration
of a name, a likeness
a look, a semblance

alliterative sun and seconds
wind tunnel, water tower
heat and hours

mimetic minutes
light and lichen
a lick that leaves

a substance—
a substantive self:
a question—

I want a trap
for the notion
of boundedness

for the boundaries
of a person
the *I* is indexical—

I points to where
the words come from—
a form, contextual

your form, lichen
is consensual
the *I* dissolves

it must wants to—
my fingertips move
over *you,* a cloud's shadow

The End of Fair Weather

I place a bundle of white feathers in a drawer.
I gather cloud slips to give to a lover.
These are among the last blue-sky days.
The continent will soon go full centigrade.
We'll throw our old clothes away.
Each day in winter is a mirror
through which one may step, overdressed,
into record-breaking summer.
It's not useless to call out
the name of a moth just gone
extinct, any more than it's useless
to sing in a dead language
while frying eggs to start the day.
As in, either it is or isn't useless.
Who here is qualified to decide?
I see the larkspur vanishing.
I see my jeans threading to skin.
In a dream, my lover tells me to start
a panic journal. I say, *I don't want these things
written down.* She sends me the ocean
in a black envelope. I see myself opening it
on a pixelated screen. I see my name
beside the word

　　　　　　　　　executor.

You, Emblazoned

Yet your voice was *here*—

        just there-here in our house, shining eyes
who dazzled twice, already timed,

a pulsing wind below the glass in spring,
and coaxed, intelligent, stoic, touching everything, you stirred
me to life, in spite of illness and damage

to the country, field laid waste, election blaze, illness
wasting a brain, a mind. Mars, and ocean, canceled.
Cream and streamers, canceled,

                    censored.
"I *am*," you said,
          though your skin flickered

to hackberry bark, or as bullet
pierced pineal gland, blinking out
your day-night clock. Your syllables

endure frail days, which blow
through equinox, dissipate, time out—

        you imagined the planet
        with you already gone:

a sad expression, no real loss, the earth still a wild salon,

yet the name you chose
is etched into air, a violent wind
parts my chest, tenderviolet, electric

nights in our sheets, no longer
countable, unrecounted. You, here, again,
my is-are-were, have-been-is, in my

arms, bed is-was our house-eyes, in my
only thought only root only *gone*,
my big *only gone* still here voice
blazing, I mourn you-her,

her-you, who were born-dreamed into the world's thicket
yet reinvented through an inner radiance,
the radiance of a name,
the name that is yours,
the radiance that is-was yours
                      that is-was you—

The Question of Surviving This

In my next life

      [since this
one turned
      to stasis
the horror

      glazed
with spring
          without her
knees

beneath
    the sheets
               ]

I live with the beetles,
invisible
      in the dark.

My grief has no witness,
a quartz in a quarantine,
      hard and common

as enforced social distance.
The rain is fearful,
      expressionless.

And I'm looking into her
like a mirror. I, too,
       am a firefly:

that spark
on the fence
       too temporary to imagine.

          I'm bright and ready,
          heaving
              to be gone

Kelly in Violet

A palimpsest, after Marosa di Giorgio's The History of Violets, *translated from the Spanish by Jeannine Marie Pitas*

> *Is it true*
> *That I have set you apart*
> *Inviolate . . .*
>
> —MINA LOY

> *the one with violets in her lap*
> *]mostly*
> *]goes astray*
>
> —SAPPHO (TRANSLATED BY ANNE CARSON)

*

I remember that night, when time was slit in two. Equinox, a
salt kiss, the door swinging. Violent light only one of us slipped
through. And the sky—March evening sky, new moon sky, black
as a gun. Winter tunneling into a spring that would never come.
And the tall trees still bare, catching red flashing lights next to the
park. And the roped-off area I could not pass.

And the next morning, lying in a bed, slips of paper floating,
names and numbers strewn. Your exquisite voice everywhere, and
nausea setting in. Tiny violets in the yard, hard as a nipple, hard
as lead.

You—

     dazzling—

   dead.

*

When I think of the past, I see burning things: amber, skin of your wrist, butter, white sugar, black sugar,

> tending this four-year fire, pines blazing and magnolias, the
> manias, avoiding public bathrooms, sweet maize, catatonia,
> an engagement of orange blossoms.

You're tall and beautiful in your flowy white jumpsuit, walking barefoot in the park, padding softly, your soft hair pulled up high, your hands laughing. The butterflies want you back, the hawks want you back, the moon is pining.

*

Nettles at Again Park, and dandelions. The path is covered and uncovered by them, like gold quilts. Again Park—why there, my love, why this

      place, this

      name? *Again* . . .

This is the pink moss moon, pandemic moon. You're barely gone. And the bats are here, with all the phlox, painted in the sky with pink wings and star eyes, in oil paints. You're hardly gone. And I won't be allowed to see your child again, your boy belongs only to his mother now. Contagion moon, mask moon—you're already gone—

      and there's a song, very quiet, in his mother's head, perceptible for an instant, then clear, then gone. In my dreams, your boy hurls his toys on the lawn, or bikes through the park, or comes into the kitchen, grabs at a bowl of shining fruit, stares at me. I look back fearfully and start to cry. He darts away running

          and running again

        into your arms, *again*—

*

This is the night of March daffodils. At ten o'clock, the hackberry
roots held you, the branches quivered, jeweled oblivion pulled
you spiraling forward. An owl's wings spoke to you, kissed you,
told you to step out of your life. You listened. Your listening
became desire. Your listening married the darkness. Your lashes
glittered with seawater.

You opened to another landscape and other beings.

I can't say if this opening was purely your illness, a delusion of
some kind, or if it was lucidity, a choice to end your suffering.

For months I was obsessed with the question.

I had to open too. I asked my ancestors for help. I asked my
father for help. Sometimes I was quiet, bewildered, humbled, and
sometimes I screamed.

I didn't dare say what I knew. I didn't say that I was dead. That
if I wanted to move forward in time, on Earth, I would be forced,
eventually, to resurrect.

I wasn't ready.

*

I don't know why, but I dream of honey, drizzled on a white plate.

Her sweetness could live forever, alongside future weddings, fountains, lakes—but then, suddenly, I see bougainvillea, *pan dulce*, and those pale pioneers, her parents. With six children in tow, always in the same clothes. Childhood's strange injuries, her disaffirming sisters.

Sometimes, in that country, the scent of rose water was cloying, and she fell sick.

Everything lives and dies under thick marigold blossoms.

*

On many nights, I went back; everything happened over and over.

                                                            I saw figures planting trees at Again Park, but this must have happened before I was born. The owl—custodian of night—soaring in the sky, watching the night. You see, time has abandoned me. Now I foresee the past, and recall what will come. My skin is burning with grief, its gems, its glinting facets. The magnolia is only truly visible at night, those cosmic branches, and blooms of wax held up by stars.

Whenever I cross this threshold of trees, I'm met by strange sounds. In the park, a disoriented moon has risen, a clock with hands whirling, changing faces.

And Kelly is still there, you know? Like a tall flower, smooth, bending in the wind, listening.

She will recognize me.

*

And in the early spring, the clouds hung under the trees, getting the street wet. It was still cold, and Grae stayed at the house with me. We didn't want summer to come. We didn't want morning to come. The sun was beautiful and starting to stream, and the trees blossomed incredibly. And we resented everything because you were gone. We kept the curtains shut. We squinted when we had to go outside. And we waited for night, when you would appear again in the space before the altar we made. And on the altar, we placed things to call you back: white and cream candles, vases with lilies overflowing, paintbrushes with your fingerprints still on them, tiny pink roses, slivers of hackberry bark, rose quartz, clear quartz, eucalyptus, chalcedony, the last book you were reading, smoky quartz, a dead ladybug, its red translucent wings. And the portrait of you, serious, with your hair down, in your sleeveless blouse, your hand on your shoulder. We talked about you while you watched from at least two places at once.

That spring the dogwood blazed—each blossom huge, perfect, without flaws—it was dreadful, a phenomenon of pink brilliance. In that field, you could hear it budding, its tremendous rumor.

It was just like the spring when I was twenty and first loved with a puzzling violence.

Even back then, I think, there was the perfume of violets.

And now the violets grew, unbridled, in my yard. I begged for a sign. And from everywhere, ladybugs arrived—the most queer, the most devoted. As if sent from some other dimension, the ladybugs came, their bodies like red beads, and heads of shiny onyx.

A gigantic one appeared on my altar table, its eyes open and calm, and lasted forever——

like a poet.

*

Last night I thought of the wooden wardrobe, my mother's, from my childhood. And my mother's earrings (the sea glass ones, imperfect), and all her necklaces. And all the old photographs, and her bowl of mold and rose petals.

A little ceramic beetle, red with black polka dots, flew from the roses to eat wedding rice from my hands.

She seemed so alive to me that I believed it, and I wanted to kiss her.

But then, I remembered that my life had burst into flames, and now I had only ashes.

*

When night falls, the neighborhood becomes desolate; I walk to the park without seeing anyone.

Connecting with another realm, I hear a voice. Under the trees, it's mostly static—notes high and whispery, like feathers brushing my ear. I realize it's more than one voice.

And those primal voices, with their unforgettable pealing, have come to tell me the tale (*again*) of a wedding turned into a wake.

And the moon, faithless, luminous in its lair of oranges.

*

My grief today is a sweater, sleeves weighted with blossoms, heavy as hematite. It poses on the bed, it flashes in the mirror; it's a wandering flame, scorching her papers, her blouses. I swear to people that she's still alive; they look at me with pity and start to cry.

A pink sweater is walking around in our house. It scares me, but I won't force it to go.

This crazy fabric is going to kill me.

*

Those tiny jars of ashes. Those tiny bottles of tinctures. Tiny
soaps, orange, lemon, and candles. And masks in all colors,
handmade and sent through the mail. And tiny bottles of hand
sanitizer by the front door. Avocados, apricots, and fresh figs,
yellow and green and gold-colored. An unthinkable number
of oils. Lavender oil, cedar oil, rosemary, eucalyptus, cypress,
peppermint, black spruce . . .

Fruit bowls and hazelnuts appear in the kitchen. Dinner appears
at the door. Red and pink and gold-colored sunsets appear each
day, unbelievably organized. Around them I'm building a house
that exists outside of time. I bring the sunset inside, hold my hand
against it to stop time. I record the hours and days in order to
prevent time from passing.

If I organize them, I can destroy them.

Then I will stay close to her.

Sometimes, on the path that stretches from our front door to the park, you appear to me.

You appear as a bouquet of white feathers, like snow or the color of paper.

At the park, in the cool air, you're fleshed out again with irises, periwinkle, dandelions. The dogs run across the field toward you; the cats are brought to their knees. You go off like a wildfire; and suddenly we're together in the kitchen again, by the stove, under the dried lilies hanging; you flick salt into the water. You glide around, you pull my hand to your new nipples. You grab my hand, pull me up and out the door; you scare the brindle dog, who howls, and an owl breaks into flight.

You say my name, and we go off behind the clouds, away from the violets who wish to comfort me, but who insist that you are gone.

*

Girls like you, you told me, are born in silence; some are born
in silence, others with a brief shriek, or soft thunder. Some are
lavender, others pink; that one is gray and looks like a dove, or the
statue of a dove; still others are gold or purple. Each one bears—
and this is what's awful—the initials of the corpse it comes from.

But, you said, it doesn't have to be this way. At some hour, and
it's different for each, the living girl arrives and starts crying, or
singing. She starts speaking. Some mothers give their permission.
Then the girl gets to choose. This name like salt crystals, a pink
name, or like velvet, a dove gray one.

Your mother didn't realize that she drove her daughter away.

She wept and grasped her breast and called out desperately for her
son.

*

I am always the same child in the shadow of my father's apartment
building. The windows are lit, I see the green curtains with
cursive stitching. The pears are gold and hard in the street, I hide
between the trees. But then, I look again toward the apartment; I
hear the conversations we had before he died, the songs playing;
I watch my sisters and half sisters arriving, and my mother, and
his other ex-wife. The voices rise over the little field behind the
complex; the voices call me in.

But I stay hidden among the leaves. The pears won't ripen. They
are like rosebuds, like sisters.

*

At night, sounds from the other world were becoming audible to me. The moon floated in the static, and I saw bats scatter over its face. The bats looked like dust motes, or eyelashes. I heard some kind of ringing.

The ringing continued. I listened in the black shadow of a maple tree. And my father—now dead more than ten years—was just sitting there in his jeans. An aleph floated above his head.

He pointed at some bright thing moving in the distant trees. I asked, is it a pink bat? I squinted, tried to get closer, he held me back. The ringing continued. I asked, is it a shooting star, injured, shifting in the branches?

But he only hinted at what it was. It is your teacher, he said. It is a poet on her deathbed.

I don't know when I realized it was Kelly.

But then, I forgot (*again*).

My father and I keep having the same conversation, over and over.

No matter what I do, I can't put the events in order.

That shooting star destroys me every time.

*

In the days after her death, violets

embraced the whole yard. My days

were smudged with the scent. The edges

of my memories, smudged with soot.

I was burning. I wasn't sure I was alive.

Spring passed. And a piercing childhood scent

flooded me; that fragrance, of roses

layered with citrus,

chlorine, honeysuckle,

mustard flowers, cement

in rain. Because of the smell

I was emboldened, like poets, pastors,

drunks, or the terminally sick.

*

I'm at the altar with Grae, we've finished lighting the candles.
And there's a strange feeling in the room, and it seems that this is
the very night when Kelly could come back—not the murderer,
not the thief who will take everything away from me, but the real
her, the lover, the cheerful intellectual.

Compelled, I go to the park. I'm afraid but desperate to see her,
and I'm greeted immediately by a swarm of ladybugs, shining like
obsidian, with little whirring voices. They tell me a story in which
Kelly traps a wild dog violet; she puts her in the middle of my life,
in the middle of a room in a chapel. The story goes on: there is
this and that animal and flower, and Kelly is busy with important
tasks.

But I keep interrupting to ask about the wild dog violet, the
chapel.

I keep asking if I can keep her. That soft-petaled creature.

*

The long blocks covered in dead leaves, their brown and pink
and orange furls; the garlic skins and the dried violets and other
mysterious flowers that came and went; the ivy tangled in the
cords and wires against the house, pulling, pulling; the wind
filling with electricity and voices of the dead; the new lives that
suddenly burst onto the scene; the gray kitten I brought home, his
gleaming fur, his eyes I could see; the blue hydrangea and purple
archangels; the orange blossom soap I found again, which smelled
like her; the frozen flour, so soft, thrown into the snow; the grass
flickering green to yellow to brown and back; memories of that
spring a dozen years ago. And the fog surrounding that time. That
first loss. Father.

*

The moon is filled with larkspur. Filled with lupine beads,
pinecones, violet light.

I light the candles, and those blue flowers called love-in-a-mist
cast spidery shadows on the wall.

The candles dance, the shadows with them.

When the moon rises, it begins nameless spells. To cast them, it
only needs a silhouette, willow charcoal, a broken watch.

In the morning, neighbors walk past with their dogs, their hearts
that beat.

I see my grandma walking by in her red dress and beads. And
Kelly, and Drake, Anne, Hunter, Eliana, James. And my father,
and my grandfather. They're all here. Though it seems to others
that there is no one.

*

The larkspur are like angels, like the dead, like me, like everyone.

The past looks me dead in the eye and I look back. In the ring I now wear,

        there

        are the bones

        of Kelly—

            still walking through this world.

*

Those first hours after, I heard people say something like, "Kelly has died and they're bringing her to Chapel _____," but since I didn't believe it, this didn't mean anything to me.

Above the tulip poplars, I saw the planets. One was huge, hanging in the sky like a severed hedge apple, like a brain or a moon. Everywhere there were ladybugs. I sensed their song at all times, signaling change, the point at which all things converge.

I stayed at the altar I'd made for her. I needed to stay there, as candlelight fell through the eucalyptus. What leaves, what shadows and light, full of strange syllables.

Finally, after three days, I did go to the chapel. I needed to go there, I begged them to bring me to her, nothing else mattered.

I can't say what happened there—not yet.

*

A few weeks passed. Then her brother, on my porch. It was Seth, the eldest. He had a gentle look on his face, sort of. And then he sobbed. And I knew his heart was broken, like mine, and I trusted him.

But then, suddenly, slowly, I started figuring things out. It was the language he used. When he said her name, it was only for me; he didn't believe it. He hadn't believed her.

Later, I ran in terror

to the park / I asked her to show me / anything /
I saw her / in the river / of her childhood / I saw her
mother / father / sisters / brothers / they surrounded her
/ they gazed into her / they were like animals piercing her
with seven pairs of green eyes / eyes of love / eyes of hurt
/ covetous eyes—

and nearly insensible, I saw her run out from their circle,
into the woods; and she came upon a yellow field; and she
floated in the dandelions, took refuge in that golden sea.
Seth found her and was coming toward her now. And she
was going to run again, but she stopped. Seth waded into
the dandelions, floated and swam there with her. Then,
wanting to comfort her, he took her hand and said, "Don't
cry. I'm taking you back home, where you belong."

I couldn't protect her.

*

Her siblings, grieving in another town. In our neighborhood, a lone water tower, and trees like dew-covered crosses. In the gauzy light of the moon, the bats began to fall asleep sweetly, as if the story would end another way. The bats yawned and blinked. Their sister had been vulnerable, but they couldn't see it; they were angry and licked their wounds.

Suddenly, I heard a voice shouting, repeating two syllables, a name that sounded something like "Kelly . . . Kelly!" I realized it was my voice. I couldn't stop shouting.

Every day, I used to tell her, "You were born here, among the irises, and you belong here." And her eyes would shine.

Who will I say these words to now?

*

Among the violets, the queer women stroll; past the patches of
daffodils like spring candy, among the fountain and honey bursts,
a lovely figure floats in violet skirts, with violet eyes, trailed by a
feral cat and city butterflies.

And the missionaries come, and they cry out, calling her by the
wrong name. "_____!"

They continue to say that name, and each time, her color
diminishes.

And her eyes are a bit sunken, two pools in the shadows.

But suddenly from her shoulder blades, brilliant red-feathered
wings burst. And her cheeks are rouged. And she turns away from
the audience, and she begins to sing.

*

I remember the morning she signed her new name at the courthouse. She was glowing.

Her name was abundant and alive and her own. It was the only thing that made her want to live.

Except on the days when suddenly they appeared to her, those angels; one looked just like her mother, and it stayed like a white bloom, fixed, in her car. We tried to get it out, but it was impossible. It taunted her, its waxen face, blue eyes, corn silk hair. Her mother's hair was everywhere.

Those angels lit their matches in every room of the house; they drew on the walls with pink and blue pencils; they unsheathed tiny daggers, like the sharpest scissors she used to crop her drawings; they gave her little cuts, on her ankles; she covered them up with socks. They stole her favorite memories.

I tried to clear the angels out, but it was hard, since I couldn't always see them.

And they would sneak back into her dresser and hide in her clothes whenever I turned around.

*

The moon was blooming, a blue violet, very sweet, and a little silver, as if it had slipped from a false outer skin. All over the world, the salt marshes of the dead were hissing, and people were losing their sense of smell. The night was surreal. It was April. Grae had come to the house, but now we stood in the small field at the corner of Ash. I smelled amber and smoke, and it was painful that the night was so lovely. That loveliness felt empty, searing. It was the hour when she would be baking an apple pie from scratch if it were fall. But I was grieving, and I was possessive of my grief, nothing else mattered to me.

I saw the redbud trees were starting to bloom; they were saving me, they were wrecking me. I saw that it had to be this way. Living things had to change, trees were replanted elsewhere, plaques left behind to do the impossible. On the other side of the park, I decided, I would gather her energy and store it. Was that possible? What choice did I have? Portals to the other world would open and close, close and open. Grae and I drank pink gin over ice and told the bats everything. New seasons opened like hollows in trees; I climbed in and hid.

*

They'd said a virus was spreading. The bustling began in March.
We set out our favorite quilts and pillows, we ate sweetbreads and
cookies in the morning, and at night, ate olives and cheese off the
cutting board. Out the window, the birds were singing, and wisps
of rain lingered by. Someone knocked on the door, but I didn't
answer; they said each household had to stay alone.

But the virus was coming—we didn't know from where. I fell
to my knees, crying; she was pacing and wanted to go out. We
weren't supposed to. She put fresh cilantro on everything; she ate
her lunch, drank, explored the house; she got bored. She declared
that she wanted to go out, but I was scared she wouldn't return.
She examined the cupboards, the drawers, replaced lightbulbs. She
played games by changing the clocks; she smelled the cinnamon
sticks and eucalyptus; she searched her closet, she tried on outfits;
she looked in the mirror; she asked who is Kelly. I said you are.

She chose.

*

Because I happened to remember it all: the park; my father's dream of a dog; that place where I grew up, on a hill; endless talks with friends in the dark; the dish of almonds; old friends and new ones; the eye shadow palette of coral, carnation, and clementine; the return from the park each evening; the milky stars; new friends who will never get to meet you; the unbearable overpass streaming with stars;

> Kelly, I remember the wedding we never had, at that park we loved in the city, under the magnolia; the sage dress you were wearing; the sage jacket I wore; my stupid crown of pomegranate. Flecks of stars.

*

She always had the reddest lips, shimmering berries.

Sometimes, before dawn, when the moon puts me in a trance,
I sleepwalk the half mile to the park, up to the nearly invisible
portal, the hackberry trunk. Each root is covered with my cries;
each teardrop is a sapphire without walls; you can see an entire life
inside.

For a year now, I've stood here in my suit, or in my nightdresses,
absorbed in memory, and I'm sure I seemed to be absorbed in
meditation, or in concentration on some birdcall.

And hearing someone new approach, I turned

toward him with a stare like a slate blue arrow.

And he didn't flee, never to return; he reached

toward me, he held me, he trembled with me

in the air, in the immense light of the moon.

*

Those first days after—how my heart raced. My blood was confused.

At first, I didn't know exactly where they had found her—she had gone out—perhaps they found her in the little field? The area was roped off; lights flashed red. Eventually—was it days later? weeks?—there she was, I sensed her, the guardian of the portal. The hackberry tree, those great roots, where she had been sitting when she died. Her face was filled with music; her cloak was the color of water; now there was no tremor in her hands. But no one said anything about her presence, instead they said she was gone. Only the little foxes started jumping, making their strange sounds at night, outside the bedroom window.

Finally, I went to see her at Chapel _____.

Her mother—and she hadn't seen her in three years—was standing by a window. I didn't say a word, but I let her walk me to the room.

She left me there.

I closed the door—

*

suddenly a brilliant red-tailed star

flew across the sky, a sun reversing time,

I crossed one world to another

I stood with her in the other world

—I crossed the room; wasn't afraid; was only scared of leaving,
of the moment ending; couldn't bear the thought of being away
from her body; her skin was cool, soft, and I knew the truth—
that I could disappear under the earth with her. The terrible thing
was that she had been pointing her gun at me from the beginning.
When she fired, I fell too; but only she was dead.

I was trembling, asking her why I had lived, why she hadn't.

I touched her face. Her arms. Her legs.

I stood there forever. I never left.

I sang to her.

I cut a lock of her hair.

I entered her death.

*

I remember the pink and heather gray sweater. And the rose of
her body, her marble shoulders, her delicate head.

And how she held her son in her mind's eye, like a mother. How
she held his beauty and didn't want to let go.

And the blue corridors of her veins. And the salt she was afraid of,
and the rubies inside her skin. And the things she would not eat:
jeweled beets, sweet yams, sparkling cucumber.

I remember the light in two rooms where we made promises, and
made love.

She said forever, and I said it.

I remember her eyes glistening, and how her footsteps paused in
the evening, downtown. How she laughed when I looked up at the
moon.

I remember the summer peaches, and the harvest apples.

And her feet in the grass, stepping lightly, to turn away.

And our friends smoking in the backyard, and the frogs singing.

I remember eternity.

*　*
*

The Question of Surviving This

By living
I am somehow, already,
in my next life—

      though I say
      I can't

      and
      I won't

      and
      I don't want to

I'm breathing,
          this can't
          be

                belabored:
                I
                am alive

and her love
plays out
in all

      of me,
      each cell—
            so,

then,
            isn't she *here*
her eyes

shining and her legs
shaved smooth
the strength in her

            shoulders
and fear at night
in her dreams

How I Became Possible

I'll fall in love again
one night in a high tide year.

I'll fall in love when the radio
plays a burning song.

This sunset residence
will always be yours,

but this California tongue
belongs to me.

I cried out, graphing
palm trees on your back.

Then fade to black,
then puff pastry,

the scent fanning out
at dawn.

Streetlamps glance the hour,
strawberries in your mouth.

Your strawberry cunt
in mine.

I amplify each memory,

play each track—

      in each room, we're still
   stretching

into each other's current—
instead of missing,

instead of your body
no longer existing.

A Year

When you died
the walls of our house
disintegrated

and all the handles
rattled and crashed
to the floor.

A gasp rushed
into the walls, adding air
with nowhere to go.

I didn't know yet, but felt the gap
of silence,
heard water carving

a canyon of absence.
I turned on a faucet
and screamed when your hair

went down the drain.

The bullet that entered
and exited your head,
leaving your face

fully intact
was not found

in the grass here,
or in the street, over there,
along the park's

edge. The sergeant said
it could be anywhere
depending on the angle

of the gun I didn't
know you had,
and there's nothing

sadder than the yellow
daffodils growing
in the yard again

a year later and how
at night their color
dies in the new moon,

that beautiful hue

is d e c e a s e d   the word
stretches out
of meaning out of time,
how your light
escaped the body
I loved,
went e l s e w h e r e

an energetic spill
I ramble looking

for signs of, a pattern
I know and can't live without
moving toward,
trying to curl
into, I
remember your light,
holding as much of it as I can
by yearning into it

Via Negativa

My grief is not the idea of *the lover*
or *nature,* not the pretty desert poppy
running late to its future,
not this photo from before
I even met her. Look, it's the Mojave
and I am thin, wearing sunglasses
and a light sweater. I sip pink champagne
with my sister, next to a rock
with the address "10,000" chalked on.
That day, my uncle came out of a trailer
and wept because we kept getting older.
He believed there was gold in the ground there
and that he had discovered anti-gravity.
He died the same year as my lover. My grief
has no gravity, no beating center, it is not alive,
not graphite or diamond, not global
pandemic or my home's dry palette
of sagebrush and fire, the smell
of the lemon grove on the hill, burnt
umber, Roman lavender,
or invasive eucalyptus, its vibrant
takeover. My grief is not Rome

or empire, though my body knows
that weather: north or south of the equator,
a specific latitude of any western shore:
sea wind in the olive trees. I'm in the Midwest
far from California and the sea and my grief
is not a death or gender
transition or the mirrors covered
for a week after. We said her bipolar
disorder was like another
human figure, like a third
person living with us, trying to drag
her light under—now everyone
talks about her
in the third person,
in the past tense,
as electricity pulses, as water rises
to float an urban center, as I float
toward the widowed future,
as icebergs circulate
on the glaciologist's monitor.

Queer Time

We're living in dead time

so many times
       before I lost her
I almost lost her

        though her skin
               was warm as wine
        in a sunned jar

and she talked about it
        how close she'd gotten
               to that threshold
        that world in which

she was already
        wind in fig tree
               shocked light
        cypress tilt   hawk light

We're living in dead time

        though I held her
               sunned shoulders
        in my two hands

the thought was here
      when she was alive
           that she could have

          already

        *

Dead time. Borrowed time. A window narrowing. A tipping point. I felt like I was watching her die. It was hardhard for others to seesee even whenwhen we tried to say

everything.
      I cherish the years we had after the first scares.

        *

    my heart is cool now
        made of discolored clay
    images flow backward
        pounding under pressure

    my knees are shunned
      blue oranges
          washing into the sea

We're living in dead time

      as common as
        uncommon
     for our kind

Narrative

I tell a friend to take it easy at the beginning of love,
even if the passion is strong.

I say this knowing how hard it is—

> *O juniper*
> *O robin in the grass*

                                        —how impossible
with some loves, some moments of life.

      From the start, you were my one violet,
a clean explosion
   into spring, five petals
                        unmooring me

from the first time we made love.
                    I think of
who we were then: our bodies different and our names,
our story not yet known, our love not even
full-grown—and you,

                  alive. Yet isn't it a mistake
to say I know our story now? Isn't that the thing?

                  I don't believe in dying
fixing—stilling—anything.

Since the night
you left,

                           I've been wading out
            into something constantly moving, not unlike the sea
               of tulips I photographed our first week together,

                                      their colors the only way I knew
                             to say what it felt like to hold you.

I tell a friend to take it easy at the beginning of love,
but in a single night,
                        my decision of *you*

was already made, like swimming back
to shore from the middle of a lake.

Grief Shift

The dream was like a moon, and someone dreamed of milk after she died. The dream was like milk, and a gallon of milk was in the car when she died. The moon was draped in cloth, a gallon of milk hanging from a thread in the black night. What a backdrop it was, night, dream, scenery, hunger. I saw her there, waiting for me to come onstage and join her and the others. She was dancing, she was buying milk. I was afraid, but I went. Or I was brave, but I knew it wasn't my time. I stayed as long as I could.

Outside, someone was waiting for me. He said we had to take the theater door. Now we were in a hurry. We had to carry it to my car, load it in the back, the trunk wouldn't close. We buckled into the journey. I craved him and my hunger was infinite. I felt something shifting, but I knew it would shift back every year.

The moon was made of fabric, cream-colored, with layers of lace. We talked about it, how the moon was uneven, lopsided, whip-smart, how my luck had caved in under a shadow. But he said he felt like she was with us, and I was happy because he knew. The door we were traveling with was painted red, like a holiday. We set off, my headlights tucking our path in. *Watch out,* he said. A cactus was growing right out of the road, low. I swerved. I swerved around more. The moments stacked up. The moments piled like cactus spines. They shone. He was wearing stripes, the headlights, the moon's lacy rays. I can't say where we were going, but I can't say that I felt only afraid.

Loving After Loss

FOR RP

when two people kissing
reinitiate each other's foundation

—MALVA FLORES (TRANSLATED BY JEN HOFER)

all night long, the curtain was pulled back
and dawn drew me toward it, through the dark hours
in which, missing you, and feeling the strangeness
of missing you along with her, I swarmed above the pages
of a book searching for a lost syntax that could lead me
to this new form of desire, desire after obliteration,
I shouldn't overstate this, the death of myself
when she died, I shouldn't overstate it:
obliteration

                    the first time I saw you
I was already held in your arms,
we held each other standing in the grass in a storm,
it was the night my basement flooded and my house
vanished do you remember how the first time
we met we were already making love
in the rain we were already walking between
two houses at dawn we were already right here

in the early summer storm and then
you were in another city and I was already
missing you the day we met and realizing
I was in love with you the day we met you were
out of town and I met you in the dream I had
of walking by your house and looking up
just as you were opening the window

    [when a lover's mouth
    reinvents a lost equation]

the first time I saw you, you were standing in the street
in front of my house and you waved hello
and said something from under your mask
the pandemic was ending soon on our block
we only had to be careful for a few more years
we didn't touch for several more years
talking all night on the porch as we grew older
looking at our watches, turning pages on calendars
the first time I saw you, you were seconds
from being inside me for the first time
the first time I saw you I was pulling you
toward me, one foot on the earth,
one in the water, one star above us the first time
I saw you I was in a field without you
with the smell of thyme, animals wading in the river,

the heat of dusk on my skin, the air soaked with dusk-light
layered with dawn-light where we met for the first time
laughing nervously because we hadn't slept
and we heard the birds beginning to fill with sound

[how a lover's voice
reignites a new sensation]

you were remarkable
we were going to make love
for the first time and we knew it, I kept seeing
you at each moment for the first time and never
wanted this to end, resisted the urge
to know the end, I want to learn a different way to
love I always want you   I always want to
see you for the first time and meet you
for the first time every time I wake up beside you
each morning resisting an anxiety I carry
under the surface of my skin because I am falling
in love for the first time and seeing you for the first
time each time I see you and I know the cost of love
and yet poured forth this wish and yet couldn't
have imagined you which is why I float in the half-night
sleepwalking with my eyes open
a sight that frightens even the animals
wading in the river and the butterflies

landing on my face who try to close my eyes for me
I tell them I'm on fire, that I carry love now
under my skin, that the love in me obliterated
me when she died and now it's rebirthing
me into myself, this my own return
to my own transmuted bedrock the way
the way we touch becomes its own occasion

94

Grief Song

I know this
      anticipation
of loss ruled
      my thoughts
not as philosophy
      but as sweat
I mean I imagined
      what animated you
gone—days the fear
      scaled seismic
a hewn place
      turned pulse
Kelly I live
      here as you
lived in the night-
      mare that startled
you awake
      I feel it too
fierce in the after-
      shocks that shift
my sense of time
      my aftermath
wading deep
      into the day
         after day

On Proliferation

We talked about birds, assemblages, hybrids.

We talked about the gap between *world with glacier*
and *world with image of glacier*.

Now I'm left in the gap between *world with you*
and *world with image of you*.

The gap between your biological life and your so-called death.
People talk about moving on, but I'm *here*,

                in the fringe,   in the expanse,

watching for you, listening for your song.
I surround myself with things that represent you,
things that *are* you.

You charge my home. Checkerbloom, paintbrush,
tea towel, jewelflower, and the dust

                of rock flour   and modern bones.

I think of your face, the image of your face, your actual face.
Every day, I talk to pictures of you.

I talk to *you*. Actual you.
You said metonymy, "when it's good,"
is more than simply language.

Change of name,
it is ontological—

     it is extension. Your existence.

You will let us in on it, if we let you.

     By perceiving you, I extend you.
     By remembering you, I extend you.
     By imagining you, I extend you.

Actual you.
I kiss you, my lips pressed flat to glass.

The Moon Is a Hen with White Feathers

*Stage directions: Read poem aloud in a room as big
as the universe. Bold text indicates a second reader
joining in, so that two voices are speaking in unison.*

On the night of loss, I watched myself dissolve
like salt into water, like sugar into a lake. **I was 37.**
And when the lake froze over, under a black and meaningless sky,
all my years had seeped into the lakebed.
Give up everything, the lake said, **you have no choice,
since everything's been taken**. I watched as my life turned
into a void, **taken**. I became nothing. I'd been living with a woman
at the edge of oblivion, and now, somehow,
unbelievably, I stood alone.
As the days and weeks and months passed,
my life became an ornate frame, a leaf-fringed emptiness,
a legend with no image, no likeness.

Slowly, that oval began to shimmer. **It began to glimmer
like someone was polishing a mirror.** I watched, I watched
it flicker. And one day when I checked, I could see myself there,
reflected back. My face. I saw that I was older, but it was the strangest
thing, **I also looked like I did at seventeen.** My eyes burning,
my hands and waist aching for comfort. **I was 38,**
but I walked outside at night, just as I did back then. **The moon
was a hen with white feathers. The moon** was a glowing flower
with petals made of crystals. I collected those crystals,
I steeped them in my tea. Every morning I drank down

the flower moon, I watched the sunrise at midnight,
I lit candles for the dawn, I collapsed the page of the day,
my past and my future folded inward,
touching at the exact point
where I moved and breathed, here, here, and **I was 39.**

Before I met you, I whispered in the grass,
lying on my back looking up at the constellations,
covered by the midwestern sky, smothered and smoldering
beneath its weight and its promise I'd survive. No—
for in the end I will die too.
The promise was that I was **alive,** now.

Before I met you Ryan
before I met you Steph and AnnElise
before I met you Marcelo and Nayomi and Lisa
before I met you Jolee and Julie and Josh
before I met you Caylin and Carly and Kieron
before I met you Sabrina and Sasha and Stefania and Vinca

The moon was so beautiful **the moon** was a freak
the moon was winter but I wasn't freezing anymore
the moon was a pillow
made of the softest crystal
I licked it like a popsicle
the moon jingled on its stem it was a flower
all the petals shook
all the petals became abstract
which triggered my hunger for something I could hold,
something I could touch again.
I held fistfuls of your hair in my sleep, and then
I was 40.

I held a note in the arctic night, the scent of cider
lifting off my lungs,
smoke in our clothes.
I held your collar and pulled.
I kissed and squeezed some cats.
I peeled an orange.
I pelted a rug.
I domesticated.
I dug a hole and hid a crystal there.
I husbanded.
I stood under the mistletoe and waited with a tiny smile.
I smelled the pines, and the pines were you.

No longer holding back,
I came back to my life. I took a vow to stay.
I wived. I opened my mouth in the rain,
like anyone would. I espoused.
I held my hands open to contain it all.
I came back to life, but not as if
I'd never left.
I didn't survive, I died.

And then, my darlings,

I revived.

The Question of Surviving This

In this, my next life

       [since that
one closed

       with a bang
the doors

       of winter
slamming

       shut
and a great

isolation
       opening
                ]

I live with a herd of cats.
I feed the softest in the dark,
she's been with me the longest,

she's the long-haired one,
the anxious,
the beautiful one.

I hold her, my skin warming
to her fur. And I'm looking into
a full moon's

face, the past
and future at once,
overlaid,

like an eclipse sliding slowly
into place. Ablaze, then bloody,
opaque.

And someone new
is here with me, his breathing
steady, this living

body
by my side
too temporary to imagine.

Around the edges
of a dark coin,
Kelly's fierce

beauty
lashes out in rays.
One day that light will carry me away

"Kelly in Violet" is an intertextual sequence, a palimp-
sest with some of the "traces" left in gray font. It is
deeply indebted to its source text, Marosa di Giorgio's
The History of Violets, translated from the Spanish by
Jeannine Marie Pitas. While grief haunts, graces, and
pervades its language, *The History of Violets* does not
seem to revolve wholly or explicitly around one specific
person's death. Di Giorgio's work, which I had read
and taught multiple times before Kelly died, opened
up new potentials for me in writing through traumatic
loss. The Catholic undertones and spiritual outgrowths
of di Giorgio's rural Uruguay, inflected with her Italian
heritage, absorbed new and different meanings, some
of them seeping from the evangelical world of Kelly's
childhood; she grew up in Mexico, speaking Spanish, a
white American missionary kid who would eventually
come out as transgender. Di Giorgio, and Pitas, helped
me access this telling.

MY THANKS

I have profound gratitude for so many—more than I can mention here—who helped me survive and made this book possible. Thank you immensely, from the depths, to my mom, Sheila Munsey; to my siblings, Genevieve Munsey, Robin Munsey, and Jen Donish; to my aunt and uncle, Lauren Stephens and Jamie Stephens; to Greg Heet; to Grae Gardiner, Micaela Bombard, Hannah Volpert-Esmond, Jacob Griffin Hall, Elijah Guerra, Eric Morris-Pusey, and Donald Quist; to Paige Webb, Miranda Popkey, Emma Wilson, Laura Bylenok, Israel Aguilar Pacheco, and Zach Savich; to all the widows in my incredible support group; to David Tager; to Jay Aquinas Thompson, Melissa Dickey, and Andy Stallings; to Mary Jo Bang, Carl Phillips, Gabe Fried, and the English Department communities at WashU and Mizzou; to the WashU students who took my grief poetry seminar in spring 2021; to Christian Kiefer, Nayomi Munaweera, Naomi Williams, Vanessa Angélica Villarreal, Marcelo Hernandez Castillo, Lisa Nikolidakis, Thomas Mira y Lopez, Dexter Booth, and the rest of the Ashland crew; to the participants of the Ladybug Salon; to Jeannine Marie Pitas; to my cats, Oakleigh and Valentine; and to Jonathan McGregor (1988–2024).

For believing in and supporting my work in crucial ways, thank you to the totally amazing Julia Eagleton; to the encouraging and brilliant Deb Garrison; to Zuleima Ugalde, Chip Kidd, and the wonderful team at Knopf; to Mary Jo Bang (again), CAConrad, Paul Tran, Joyelle McSweeney, Diane Seuss, and Daniel Borzutzky, for the extraordinary generosity of time and words; and to Eddie Powers, avid poetry reader who raised me.

To Ryan: thank you for your love, for making space for Kelly and loving her even though you never got to meet her, and for joining me in this timeline.

*

I wrote this work while living on the unceded ancestral lands of the Osage Nation, Otoe-Missouria, Očeti Šakowin (Sioux), Kickapoo, Kaskaskia, Illini-Peoria, Sac & Fox, and other Indigenous peoples who were unjustly and forcibly displaced and dispossessed. The ongoing legacies of settler colonialism continue today, and I am both complicit in them and committed to dismantling them. I am still learning.

Liberation must be collective.

Palestine will be free.

ACKNOWLEDGMENTS

The following journals published earlier drafts of these poems, sometimes under other titles:

The American Poetry Review:
>"The End of Fair Weather"
>"Nightmare at Cold Moon Resort"
>"The Question of Surviving This"

Bear Review: "Queer Time"

COMP: an interdisciplinary journal:
>"On Proliferation"
>"Agate Beach, Lopez Island"
>"Via Negativa"
>"Loving After Loss"

Denver Quarterly: "Similitude"

echoverse: "Anticipation of Spring"

The Missouri Review: "Via Negativa"

The Offing: "Dignity"

Poem-a-Day: "You, Emblazoned"

The Texas Review:

> "Grief Song"
> "Sitting in Again Park, Columbia, Missouri"
> "A Year"
> "How I Became Possible"

A NOTE ABOUT THE AUTHOR

Queer poet and writer CASS DONISH was born and raised in the Greater Los Angeles area. They are the author of the poetry collections *Beautyberry* and *The Year of the Femme*, winner of the Iowa Poetry Prize, as well as the nonfiction chapbook *On the Mezzanine*. Their work has appeared in *The American Poetry Review*, *Denver Quarterly*, *The Gettysburg Review*, *Guernica*, *The Iowa Review*, *The Kenyon Review*, *Poem-a-Day*, *Vice*, and elsewhere. Donish received an MA in cultural geography from the University of Oregon, an MFA in poetry from Washington University in St. Louis, and a PhD in English and creative writing from the University of Missouri. They live in Columbia, Missouri.

A NOTE ON THE TYPE

This book is set in Fournier, a font designed by Pierre-Simon Fournier *le jeune* (1712–1768). In 1764 and 1766 he published his *Manuel typographique*, a treatise on the history of French types and printing and the measurement of type by the point system. Fournier's type is considered transitional in that it drew its inspiration from the old style, yet was ingeniously innovational, providing for an elegant, legible appearance. In 1925 his type was revived by the Monotype Corporation of London.

Composed by North Market Street Graphics,
Lancaster, Pennsylvania

Printed and bound by LSC Communications,
Crawfordsville, Indiana

Book design by Pei Loi Koay